Play Ball, Snoopy

Selected cartoons from
Win A Few, Lose A Few, Charlie Brown, Vol 1

Charles M. Schulz

CORONET BOOKS
Hodder Fawcett, London

Copyright © 1973, 1974 by
United Feature Syndicate, Inc.

This book comprises the first half of
WIN A FEW, LOSE A FEW, CHARLIE BROWN.

First published by Fawcett Publications Inc.

Coronet edition 1978

Printed in Great Britain for
Hodder Fawcett Ltd., Mill Road, Dunton Green,
Sevenoaks, Kent (Editorial Office:
47 Bedford Square, London WC1 3DP) by
C. Nicholls & Company Ltd,
The Philips Park Press, Manchester

ISBN 0 340 22951 9

PLAY BALL, SNOOPY

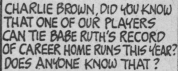

SNOOPY CAN TIE BABE RUTH'S HOME-RUN RECORD?

BUT I THOUGHT HANK AARON WAS GOING TO DO THAT...

SNOOPY'S AHEAD OF HIM!

SNOOPY ONLY NEEDS ONE MORE HOME RUN! HE CAN TIE BABE RUTH'S RECORD BEFORE HANK AARON IF THE PRESSURE DOESN'T GET TO HIM...

PRESSURE? WHAT PRESSURE?

HERE, YOU GOT A LETTER..

"DEAR STUPID, WHO DO YOU THINK YOU ARE TRYING TO BREAK BABE RUTH'S RECORD?"

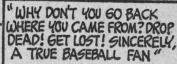

"WHY DON'T YOU GO BACK WHERE YOU CAME FROM? DROP DEAD! GET LOST! SINCERELY, A TRUE BASEBALL FAN"

IS IT FROM ANYONE YOU KNOW?

ONE OF MY ADMIRERS

BABE RUTH HIT SEVEN HUNDRED AND FOURTEEN HOME RUNS...

THAT HAS TO BE ONE OF THE MOST FANTASTIC RECORDS IN THE HISTORY OF SPORTS...

BUT SNOOPY HAS HIT SEVEN HUNDRED AND THIRTEEN HOME RUNS! HE ONLY NEEDS ONE MORE TO TIE THE RECORD...

JUST A LITTLE OL' COUNTRY BOY DOIN' HIS JOB!

STRIKE THREE!

DON'T WORRY, SNOOPY, YOU'LL GET TO BAT AT LEAST TWO MORE TIMES...

BY THE WAY, TEETH MARKS ARE NOT GOOD FOR YOUR BAT...

ALL RIGHT, SNOOPY, IT'S THE NINTH INNING...

THIS WILL BE YOUR LAST TIME AT BAT THIS SEASON...IF YOU'RE GOING TO TIE BABE RUTH'S HOME-RUN RECORD, YOU'VE GOT TO DO IT NOW!

CHARLIE BROWN'S ON SECOND... A HOME RUN WILL TIE THE RECORD AND WIN THE GAME! IT'S HERO TIME, SNOOPY!!

I JUST WANT TO BE A CREDIT TO MY BREED!

I'M SORRY, SNOOPY...I KNOW I SPOILED YOUR CHANCE TO TIE BABE RUTH'S RECORD...

BUT I ALSO DON'T THINK YOU SHOULD GET SO MAD AT ME... AFTER ALL, I'M STILL YOUR MASTER... YOU'RE MY DOG...

JUST REMEMBER, ONE LITTLE PHONE CALL AND I COULD HAVE YOU SENT RIGHT BACK WHERE YOU CAME FROM!

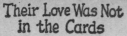

Gentlemen, I have just completed my new novel.

It is so good, I am not even going to send it to you.

Why don't you just come and get it?

Gentlemen,

Yesterday, I waited all day for you to come and get my novel and to publish it and make me rich and famous.

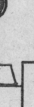

You did not show up.

Were you not feeling well?

Gentlemen,

Well, another day has gone by and you still haven't come to pick up my novel for publication.

Just for that, I am going to offer it to another publisher.

Nyahh! Nyahh! Nyahh!

Theme: Our School

Going to our school is an education in itself which is not to be confused with actually getting an education.

I DON'T NEED THAT KIND OF TROUBLE!

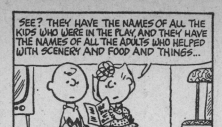

SEE? THEY HAVE THE NAMES OF ALL THE KIDS WHO WERE IN THE PLAY, AND THEY HAVE THE NAMES OF ALL THE ADULTS WHO HELPED WITH SCENERY AND FOOD AND THINGS...

WHERE DO YOU COME IN?

WHERE DO I COME IN? JUST READ THAT LAST LINE... YOU'LL SEE...

"SPACE DOES NOT PERMIT THE LISTING OF ALL THOSE WONDERFUL PEOPLE WHO GAVE THEIR TIME AND EFFORT WHEN NEEDED"

BY GOLLY, DON'T TELL ME I'M NOT IMPORTANT ENOUGH TO GET MENTIONED!

I'M COMPLETELY CONVINCED!

THE DOG IS REGARDED AS THE FRIEND OF MAN...

THIS PARTICULAR BREED IS GENERALLY QUITE GENTLE AND THIS PARTICULAR DOG IS BOTH GENTLE AND INTELLIGENT...

ALTHOUGH HE DOES HAVE HIS FAULTS...

SUCH AS FLIRTING WITH THE GIRL IN THE FRONT ROW!!!

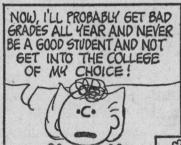

SSSSSS!!

His wife had always hated his work.

"You'll never make any money growing toadstools," she complained.

"On the contrary," he declared. "My toadstool business is mushrooming!"

She creamed him with the electric toaster.

"Do you love me?" she asked.
"Of course," he said.

"Do you really love me?" she asked.
"Of course," he said.

"Do you really really love me?" she asked.
"No," he said.

"Do you love me?" she asked.
"Of course," he said.
So she asked no more.

GOOD MORNING, MISS... I'M SELLING A NEW ITEM FOR KITTENS, AND I..

FOR WHAT?

FOR KITTENS...THIS IS A NEW TOY I HAVE DEVELOPED...A KITTEN CAN ENTERTAIN HIMSELF FOR HOURS WITH THIS TOY...

THE TOY IS SIMPLICITY ITSELF... I HAVE TAKEN SEVERAL PIECES OF SCRAP PAPER AND I HAVE CRUMPLED THEM UP...

A KITTEN WILL PLAY FOR HOURS WITH A PIECE OF CRUMPLED PAPER! HE'LL BAT IT, AND HE'LL JUMP AT IT...

AND IF YOU HANG IT FROM A STRING, HE'LL HIT IT AND BOX WITH IT AND EVERYTHING!

IT'S REALLY FUN TO WATCH A KITTEN BOUNCE AROUND...

WOULD YOU LIKE TO BUY ONE? THEY'RE ONLY FIVE CENTS APIECE..

WHY SHOULD I BUY ONE? WHY CAN'T I JUST CRUMPLE A PIECE OF PAPER MYSELF?

ALL ALONG I'VE BEEN AFRAID THERE WAS SOMETHING WRONG WITH THIS IDEA...

I DON'T KNOW WHAT'S WRONG WITH MY PASS RECEIVER...HE KEEPS COMPLAINING ABOUT HEADACHES...

WHERE WILL YOU SLEEP WHILE YOU'RE AT CHUCK'S HOUSE, SIR?

IN THE GUEST ROOM, OF COURSE!

I'M SURE THEY HAVE A GUEST ROOM... CHUCK'S DAD IS A BARBER... BARBERS ARE RICH..

ONCE YOUR SCISSORS AND YOUR COMB ARE PAID FOR, THE REST IS ALL PROFIT!

I DON'T THINK YOU KNOW MUCH ABOUT BARBERS, SIR...

STOP CALLING ME "SIR"!

GOOD NIGHT, PATTY... SLEEP WELL!

THANKS, CHUCK...I JUST HOPE THAT OL' SNOOP UP THERE DOESN'T SNORE TOO LOUD...

BEFORE YOU GO TO SLEEP, OL' PAL, HOW ABOUT TURNING OFF THE MOON?

YES, MA'AM...I'D LIKE TO TRANSFER TEMPORARILY TO YOUR SCHOOL...

MY DAD IS OUT OF TOWN, YOU SEE, AND I'M STAYING IN CHUCK'S GUEST COTTAGE SO I'LL BE GOING TO THIS SCHOOL FOR AWHILE IF YOU'LL HAVE ME...OKAY?

I'M NO GREAT SCHOLAR, YOU UNDERSTAND, BUT I'M ALWAYS IN THERE TRYING...

IF IT'S "TRUE OR FALSE" OR "MULTIPLE CHOICE," I'LL BE IN THERE WITH THE BEST OF 'EM !

MOTORCYCLE NEWS... FOOTBALL STORIES...WRESTLING ANNUAL... FISHING GUIDE...GLIDER NEWS...

..MOUNTAIN CLIMBING DISPATCH... DIRT-BIKE REPORT...BACK-PACKER'S GUIDE...HORSEMAN'S ROUND-UP...

I'M HAVING ALL MY MAIL FORWARDED HERE, CHUCK

NO, MA'AM...I DIDN'T GET MY REPORT WRITTEN BECAUSE I SLEPT IN THE RAIN ALL NIGHT!

I TRIED TO WRITE IT THIS MORNING, BUT MY HAIR WAS WET AND THE WATER KEPT DRIPPING DOWN ON THE PAPER

WHY DIDN'T I DO IT THE NIGHT BEFORE? BECAUSE THERE ARE NO LIGHTS!

ASK CHUCK ABOUT HIS STUPID GUEST COTTAGE!!!

I THOUGHT THAT STAYING AT CHUCK'S HOUSE WOULD BE A REAL EXPERIENCE

I THOUGHT THEY WERE LIKE MAYBE, YOU KNOW, THE BEAUTIFUL PEOPLE! **HA!** ALL THEY EVER DO IS WATCH **TV**!!

AND I THOUGHT THEY'D HAVE A NICE GUEST COTTAGE...**HA!** IT LOOKS MORE LIKE A DOG HOUSE! I EVEN HAD TO SHARE IT WITH THAT FUNNY-LOOKING KID WITH THE BIG NOSE!

I SUPPOSE YOU REALLY CAN'T BLAME CHUCK FOR WHAT YOU THOUGHT, CAN YOU, SIR?

STOP CALLING ME "SIR"!

"Our love will last forever," he said.

"Oh, yes, yes, yes!" she cried.

"Forever being a relative term, however," he said.

She hit him with a ski pole.

The last car drove away.
It began to rain.

And so our hero's life
ended as it had begun...
a disaster.

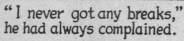

"I never got any breaks,"
he had always complained.

He had wanted to be rich.
He died poor. He wanted
friends. He died friendless.

He wanted to be loved. He
died unloved. He wanted
laughter. He found only tears.

He wanted applause. He received
boos. He wanted fame. He found
only obscurity. He wanted
answers. He found only questions.

I'M HAVING
A HARD TIME
ENDING THIS..

➡

I'M DOOMED!

I HAVE TO WRITE A REPORT ON RIVERS AND IT'S DUE NEXT WEEK, AND I JUST KNOW I'LL GET A FAILING GRADE!

WHY DON'T YOU WORK REAL HARD AND TURN IN THE BEST REPORT THAT YOU CAN POSSIBLY WRITE?

THAT NEVER OCCURRED TO ME!

"CLOSE DANCING" IS COMING BACK!

DO FALLING LEAVES MAKE YOU FEEL SAD?

ABSOLUTELY NOT! IF THEY WANT TO FALL, I SAY LET 'EM FALL!

IN FACT, FALLING LEAVES ARE A GOOD SIGN...

IT'S WHEN YOU SEE THEM JUMPING BACK ONTO THE TREES THAT YOU'RE IN TROUBLE!

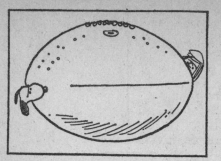

NOPE!

I'D LIKE TO HAVE YOU ON MY TEAM, CHUCK, BUT I JUST DON'T THINK YOU'RE GOOD ENOUGH...

IN FACT, I DON'T SEE ANYONE AROUND HERE WHO COULD COME UP TO MY STANDARD!

HOW ABOUT MY LINEBACKER OVER THERE? HE'S PRETTY GOOD

HIM?

OKAY, LET'S TRY HIM OUT..

➡

THE RAIN FALLS ON THE JUST AND THE UNJUST

THAT'S A GOOD SYSTEM!

THIS IS A TERRIBLE PROGRAM...
WE SHOULD SWITCH CHANNELS

CLICK!

THAT WAS PRETTY GOOD
CONSIDERING HE NEVER
EVEN WOKE UP!

This is my report on rain. Rain is water which does not come out of faucets.

If it were not for rain, we would not get wet walking to school and get a sore throat and stay home which is not a bad idea.

Rain was the inspiration for that immortal poem, "Rain, rain, go away. Come again some other day."

After a storm, the rain goes down the drain which is where I sometimes feel my education is also going. End of report

She wanted to live
in Canada.

He wanted to live
in Mexico. Thus,
they parted.

Years later, when
asked the reason,
she replied simply,

"I just didn't like
his latitude!"

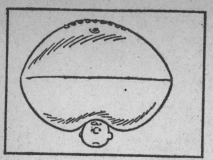

ZIP!

➤

THINGS LIKE THAT COULD RUIN SPECTATOR SPORTS...

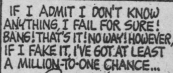

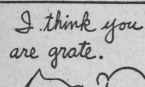

Book One
Part I
Chapter One
Page 1.

WHAT A GREAT START!

➡

ALL THIS AND SNOOPY TOO

All these books are available at your local bookshop or newsagent, or can be ordered direct from the publisher. Just tick the titles you want and fill in the form below.

Prices and availability subject to change without notice.

CORONET BOOKS, P.O. Box 11, Falmouth, Cornwall.

Please send cheque or postal order, and allow the following for postage and packing:

U.K. – One book 22p plus 10p per copy for each additional book ordered, up to a maximum of 82p.

B.F.P.O. and EIRE – 22p for the first book plus 10p per copy for the next 6 books, thereafter 4p per book.

OTHER OVERSEAS CUSTOMERS – 30p for the first book and 10p per copy for each additional book.

Name...

Address..

....